TRANSFORMATIONAL LIFE COACHING

THE TEXTBOOK FOR COACH TRAINING
Values | Culture | Evidence Based | Skills | Leadership

Dr. Carletta N. Artis

Kendall Hunt
publishing company

Cover design by Willie Latham. © Kendall Hunt Publishing Company.
Scripture taken from the New King James Version. Copyright © 1982 by Thomas Nelson, Inc. Used
by permission. All rights reserved.

Kendall Hunt
p u b l i s h i n g   c o m p a n y
www.kendallhunt.com
Send all inquiries to:
4050 Westmark Drive
Dubuque, IA 52004-1840

Copyright © 2022 by Dr. Carletta N. Artis

Text Book ISBN 978-1-7924-9523-6
eBook ISBN 978-1-7924-9522-9

Published in the United States of America

Contents

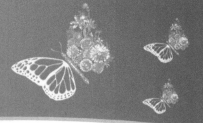

Introduction

Values

Transformational Life Coaching

Transformational coaching is the process of partnering with someone to support them through a significant change that helps them grow, develop, and ultimately "rewrite their reality." The underlying premise behind transformational coaching is that you will examine everything that could be in service of that transformation. It includes a holistic examination of your life, such as your cultural identity, influencers, and messaging that may be a catalyst or hindrance to significant change.

Transformational coaching is very different from transitional, goal-oriented, or situational coaching where the coach works with you to address a specific challenge with a focused outcome. This often happens in professional environments. A transitional coach would help you move from one job to another, while a *transformational* coach empowers you to completely rethink what's possible for you professionally. They may even help you rewrite the parameters of what a professional life could look like in the context of your whole life.

This confusion spills over into the coaching world as well, with some coaches calling what they do 'transformational coaching' when it is, often by their own definition, something else. Take, for instance, this definition which I came across: "Transformational coaching involves interactions with a coach for the purpose of increasing a coaching client's effectiveness, performance, personal development, and growth." This is an accurate description of *all* coaching; there is no form of coaching that does not endeavor to increase a person's effectiveness, performance, development, or growth. Here is another inaccurate definition of transformational coaching: "the art of assisting people to enhance their effectiveness in a way they feel helped." Again, this is a general description of all forms of coaching.

In simple terms, transformational coaching is focused on enabling *self-actualization*. Far more than 'options-strategy-action' to attain goals or clarity or to get better at something, transformational coaching dives deep into an individual's psyche, focusing on who that person is and desires to *become*. Transformational coaching is therefore an ontological approach because it is about 'being' rather than 'doing.'

The great transformational coaching question is therefore, *"Who do you choose to be?"* and what makes the process transformational is learning and doing what it takes to grow into the embodiment of that choice in being.

People will still bring their personal goals, objectives, and high dreams to the table in transformational coaching conversations; however, both coach and client are aware that those function as the *context* for the deeper dive within, and are not the end game in themselves. The driving question remains grounded in a choice in being: Who do I need to be in order for my goals or dreams to become a reality? The 'becoming' process is the transformational path, and the end game is the embodiment of higher than realized levels of existence.

How To Find and Choose a Transformational Coach

Finding and selecting a transformational coach can be an opportunity to begin building your awareness about what's important to you. As the coaching profession continues to grow, you may find friends, family, and colleagues mentioning their work with a coach. Some may even enthusiastically recommend their coach. If you don't receive inspiring referrals, other resources for locating a great transformational coach include the International Coach Federation and Masterpiece Coaching and Consultation LLC with the Author.

What Skills and Training do Transformational Coaches Receive?

A truly great transformational coach possesses a combination of knowledge, skills, and attributes that work together to drive that transformative experience for clients. Professional coaches undergo hundreds of hours of training and supervision, and usually possess a credential from a globally recognized coaching association, such as the International Coach Federation. Great transformational coaches are also life-long learners who continuously invest in their development and explore different philosophies and techniques so they can better serve their clients.

Transformative Coaching Skills:

- Whether working as a life coach, executive coach, career coach or integrating with other forms of work, Transformative coaching is about bringing zest, calm, verve, and creativity into everyday life and realizing potential. A good Transformational Coach won't shy away from the uncomfortable because it is in the uncomfortable that transformation can really occur.

- Deep listening. Absorbing all stimuli, the coach is aware of both what is being said and that which remains unsaid

- Holding space. The coach will create a safe environment for the client to fully open up, using silence as a tool for greater client introspection.

- Observing and identifying. Deeply seeing the client's beliefs and patterns of behavior, both transactionally and what lies below the surface

- Reflecting back. Sharing significant information with the client from what the coach has heard, seen and felt in the session

- Challenge. Where relevant the coach will ask the difficult question to elicit change through bringing into the space what isn't being said.

> *"Transformative coaching creates the space for the client to see themselves afresh."*
>
> *—Nick Bolton, Founder, Animas*

Transformative coaching is:

- Psychological – It explores the client both inside and out, their beliefs, values, expectations, assumptions and psychological patterns that guide how they show up in life or the workplace

- Humanistic – It builds on the assumption that clients are whole, unbroken and they have the resources they need to make changes

- Integrative – Drawn from a wide range of schools of thought, it enables coaches to find their own unique, psychologically grounded way of working with clients

- Holistic – Coaches learn to pay attention to all aspects of a client's experience – the cognitive, affective, somatic, relational and behavioral dimensions.

A Transformative Coach might similarly start with goal setting and a sense of the ideal outcome. The work would likely progress differently, however. In broad terms, in the transformational coaching space a coach is much more likely to explore a client's view of the world, view of self and their relationships. This will involve looking at their current set of assumptions around things that matter most to them, their beliefs, their values, their use of language and what this reveals around their view of the world, the stories that have been created in their lives and how this affects how they live. Thus, a Transformative Coach provides a space to improve a person's self-awareness and to see themselves afresh. This root-cause approach in turn can help to facilitate profound change in the client's lives, more so than in other traditional forms of life coaching.

What are the Benefits of Transformational Coaching?

The biggest benefit of transformational coaching is long-lasting, sustainable change. Since the process prioritizes a true understanding of the question at hand in the context of one's whole life, it offers a special opportunity. You gain awareness of the impact of your unique perspective, an understanding of the special gifts you have to share with the world and conquer fears so you can become the person you were meant to be.

While long-lasting, sustainable change is the biggest benefit, there are many other rewarding outcomes from embarking on a transformational coaching journey such as:

- Envisioning what is truly possible without compromise

- Gaining awareness about your talents, motivators, dreams, fears, cultural influences, and assumptions, then exploring how they are shaping your worldview

- Shifting to an empowered perspective and mindset
- Realizing that success does not happen in isolation, but by having support through your transformational journey
- Defining what fulfillment looks like
- Designing your own terms for success and happiness

Types of Coaching

Life coaching is defined as *"a dynamic interaction that facilitates the learning, development, and performance of the person being coached"*. It is a way to promote balance and harmony by supporting clients in living to their fullest potential. While there is enormous variability in terms of counseling approaches, one crucial distinction between coaches and counselors is that the former is not focused on a problem or diagnosis.

Instead, coaching is aimed at enhancing existing capabilities. It is a solution-focused approach in which clients are guided toward achieving outcomes.

In other words, a good coach understands that *"The will to win, the desire to succeed, the urge to reach your full potential… these are the keys that will unlock the door to personal excellence"* (Confucius).

While many coaches may adhere to a common objective, the way they get there is unique to the coach's particular background, style, and philosophical model.

"Coaching is a reflective learning process."

While the focus behind the coaching differs, all coaching is typically reflective rather than directive in manner. The Business coaching category includes executive, career and skills coaching. Relationship coaching focuses on everything from communication through to stress management and emotional wellness, such that it is a mix between personal and work life.

The intended result of a coaching process is to enable you to better achieve success in one of more areas of your personal and/or work life. And life coaching focuses on personal outcomes.

5 Types of Coaching Unpacked

1. Executive Coaching

Those in leadership positions are targeted by executive coaching, such as senior managers and directors, where performance development is a key concern. It is also called leadership or performance coaching.

The focus of Executive Coaching is:

- Enhancing performance
- Taking talents and abilities to a new level
- Helping someone to adjust to new situations or a transition
- Within one-on-one sessions, clients are afforded an opportunity to reflect and develop a personal awareness of their strengths and work on weaknesses or specific issues they find challenging. This process can be a powerful platform for improving performance in work environments.

2. Career Coaching

Career coaching is for anyone who is just starting out on a career or years into one and wants to advance or make changes in their career.

The focus of Career Coaching is:

- Skills assessment
- Understanding the job market
- Understanding organizational processes
- Identifying opportunities and career-based roles that are "good fits"
- Developing career transition plans
- The career coaching process helps clients understand the world of work and their own personal development. Within this space, coaches assist clients in establishing a career action place with, the intent of enhancing employability.

3. Skills Coaching

Aiding the enhancement of existing performance through attaining set deliverables and goals, Skills Coaching focuses on:

- Identifying and refining career goals
- Flagging objectives within existing roles

- Recognizing personal and career development needs
- Upskilling to enable better performance linked to achieving specific tasks
- Skills coaching sessions involve one-on-one programs, which are tailored to a specific individual's knowledge, experience, maturity and ambition. The focus is on achieving both individual and company objectives. The coaches who run these programs, typically possess qualifications and experience in the areas in which the skills-transfer coaching is offered.

4. Relationship Coaching

Relationship coaching aims to assist individuals, couples and groups build healthier and more fulfilling relationships.

The focus of Relationship Coaching is to address existing or potential challenges in relationships by:

- Questioning assumptions
- Identifying behavioral patterns
- Setting clear and healthy relationship boundaries
- Uncovering new listening mechanisms
- Assisting with ways to better express feelings and views
- Those embarking on this type of coaching will work through conflict resolution and effective communication techniques, stress management and ways to augment their emotional wellness.

5. Personal Life Coaching

This type of coaching intends to support individuals who wish to make some form of significant change happen in their lives.

Personal Life coaches help clients to:

- Explore what they want in life
- Define attainable dreams and aspirations

- Find answers and ways to achieve their goals
- Highlight and understand their own potential, skills and talents

"Coaching will enable you to discoverand utilize your strengths."

This type of coaching assists individuals to discover answers based on their own values, preferences, and perspectives. It is a more reflective than directive process, which attempts to instill knowledge by asking questions and challenging clients to find answers from within themselves.

"Coaching can be focused on career or personal, or both."

The coaching leadership style is about inspiring your team, building their confidence, and teaching them the skills they need in order to develop and work together successfully while ensuring they feel supported by the coaching leader along the way.

It relies on the coaching leader having good communication and social skills - as constructive feedback is important in this leadership style - but the most successful coach will also ask questions of their employees to encourage brainstorming and problem-solving.

Coaching methods can be an effective way to tackle a workplace culture that feels at best unproductive and at worst, failing. With a strong focus on goals, personal and group development, and outcomes, the results often speak for themselves.

It's also worth noting that different people respond to different management cues: tapping into the different coaching styles will impact positively on your team's performance and development, helping them achieve their goals.

Life Purpose

Life purpose is defined as having set goals and a direction for one's life (Hill et al., 2010). Many of us think of life purpose and meaning in life as the same thing, but they are slightly different. More specifically, it's thought that life purpose, or engaging in purpose-driven behaviors, is just one thing that contributes to a meaningful life.

When you have purpose in your life, you likely feel good about the way you are living your life. You might feel that there is some ultimate reason for your actions and that you are contributing to the world in some important way. This gives you a sense of satisfaction and connectedness which can help you reach higher levels of well-being.

How Do You Define Life Purpose?

Life purpose means different things to different people. One study suggests that there are four different types of purpose (Hill et al., 2010).

These types are:

- *Prosocial.* Defined as a propensity to help others and influence the societal structure
- *Creative.* Defined as artistic goals and a propensity for originality
- *Financial.* Defined as goals of financial well-being and administrative success
- *Personal recognition.* Defined as one's desire for recognition and respect from colleagues

People vary on how much they pursue each of these types of purpose. But if our goal is to increase happiness and well-being, then focusing our efforts on the prosocial type of purpose is the best strategy.

Purpose will be unique for everyone; what you identify as your path may be different from others. What's more, your purpose can actually shift and change throughout life in response to the evolving priorities and fluctuations of your own experiences.

Purpose can guide life decisions, influence behavior, shape goals, offer a sense of direction, and create meaning. For some people, purpose is connected to vocation—meaningful, satisfying work. For others, their purpose lies in their responsibilities to their family or friends. Others seek meaning through spirituality or religious beliefs. Some people may find their purpose clearly expressed in all these aspects of life.

Your life purpose consists of the central motivating aims of your life—the reasons you get up in the morning.

Finding a Life Purpose

So how do you find your life purpose (or purposes)? First, it's important to keep in mind that you can have more than one purpose. You can have lots, and the more the better. To start finding your purposes, ask yourself these questions:

1. *What pain, injustice, or problem do you really want to be solved?*

   This question can help you discover what really matters to you. Once you know this, start setting goals and intentions for how you'll help solve this problem. This doesn't have to be anything big. For example, if you really want the world to be a nicer place, you can start making it that way by practicing random acts of kindness in your daily life.

2. *What activities energize you?*

   Your answer to this question can further point to your life purpose because when you are in alignment with your life purpose, you feel energized and may even experience the state of flow—an experience where you're so immersed in what you're doing that you become fully present and may even lose track of time.

3. *What are you willing to sacrifice for?*

   The things that give us life purpose are usually the things that matter so much to us that we're willing to sacrifice other important things like leisure time or money. So what are the things, people, or projects that you're are willing to sacrifice for?

4. *Who do you want to help?*

The thing about happiness is that if we become overly focused on ourselves and our own happiness, we're actually less happy (Ford et al., 2014). That's why it's so important to disconnect for a moment from your desire to find your purpose. Instead, shift your focus onto how you can help others. Ask yourself who can you help, how can you help, and who do you want to help? Start small if you need to—offer to help a friend, give a compliment, bake cookies for your coworkers, or say thanks to the store clerk. Figuring out how you can help others in ways that are meaningful to you is the key to finding life purpose.

What Else Gives People Life Purpose?

These seven things can further contribute to life purpose:

Social Connection. Creating meaningful connections with others is a great way to increase life purpose while also boosting health and happiness.

Achievement. Achieving important goals, especially purpose-driven goals, is helpful for enhancing purpose.

Self-expression. Expressing ourselves, our emotions, our opinions, and ideas is helpful for purpose.

Excitement. Fun, joy, and excitement help life feel more enjoyable and purposeful.

Impact. When we positively impact the lives of others, we boost our sense of purpose.

Personal growth. When we work on improving ourselves in ways that matter to us, we can increase our sense of purpose.

Recognition. Admiration can give us a feeling that we are valued and are living a life of purpose.

What Life Purpose Feels Like

Finding your purpose feels a lot like finding yourself. You know who you are, what you are meant to do, and nothing can stop you from doing it. You might suddenly not care what other people think because you're doing something so important to you that no one could convince you otherwise. And pursuing your purpose doesn't require that you be successful because it's the journey that matters more than the destination.

However, our choices and actions also really matter. In some ways, this is a mystery we can't fully understand, but that doesn't mean it's not true. We can choose to do things that will bring us more joy and give us more of a sense of purpose.

In one sense, you are always living in God's purpose. God is God and He works all things, including your life, according to his purposes. Nothing can happen without God ordaining it.

Psalm 57:2 says, *"I cry out to God Most High, to God who fulfills his purpose for me."* This is key in understanding God's purpose for your life. God has numbered your days and will fulfill every purpose He has for you.

If you go about your days experiencing little fulfillment, you may be wandering from your God-given purpose. Fulfillment comes from doing rewarding, meaningful, purposeful things. And If you don't know God's purpose for your life, you constantly feel a sense of aimlessness. You feel as though you're wandering from thing to thing without any forward progress.

Here are 6 ways to discover God's purpose for your life (Ward, 2017).

Go To God In Prayer.

Again, let's start with the obvious. If you feel purposeless, ask God to give you wisdom and direction. James 1:5 states, "If any of you lacks wisdom, let him ask God, who gives generously to all without reproach, and it will be given him."

That's incredibly good news. God wants to give you a purpose. He wants to bestow divine wisdom on you. It's not like God is holding out on you to make you miserable. He desires you to have a joyful, ambitious, purposeful life. Ask God for purpose and expect Him to give it to you.

Dig Into God's Word.

The primary way God speaks to us is through the Bible. This means that one of the first things you should do in your search for God's purpose is to start digging into scripture. Now, you won't find any verses that tell you to become a dance instructor or painter, but you will begin to understand the heart of God.

Psalm 119:105 says, "Your word is a lamp to my feet and a light to my path." God's word brings light to paths that otherwise seem dark. In the Bible you learn how to live wisely in God's world, which is the first step toward finding your purpose.

Determine Your Gifts And Strengths.

God has given you very specific gifts and strengths. Maybe you're a math whiz or a wise counselor. Maybe you have a mind for electronics or business. Maybe you're great at organizing people and getting things done. God's purpose for you probably involves the things you're already good at.

This is where education can be particularly valuable. Going to college or going back to college allows you to discover your gifts and then determine how you're going to use them. It also connects you with people who want to help you find your purpose.

Determine Your Passions.

What is one thing you're particularly passionate about? Really, this can be anything. Business, art, economics, alleviating poverty, whatever. If money wasn't an issue, what would you love to do?

Determining your passions often helps you figure out what God has called you to do. It's often said that God works at the intersection of our gifts and our passions. Where do your gifts meet your passions? That may be God's purpose for you.

Bring Others Into Your Life.

Proverbs 11:14 says, "Where there is no guidance, people fall, but in an abundance of counselors there is safety." In other words, one of the main ways God will help you find your purpose is through others.

A caveat needs to be made here. Your counselors should be people you trust. Whether this is your professors, parents or friends, it needs to be people who have your back and want the best for you. You want wise counselors to help you find God's purpose for you.

Take A Solitude Retreat.

Sometimes it can be incredibly helpful to get away from it all and take some unhurried time to think, pray and journal. You don't have to spend a week in the woods for this to be effective. Even just a day away from the hustle and grind can be hugely rewarding.

During these retreats, allow yourself to simply be still. To ponder. To ask God for direction and listen for His voice. This doesn't need to be complicated and doesn't require any elaborate rituals. Hebrews 11:6 is a reminder that God always rewards those who seek him. He's not hiding in the dark, trying to keep his will hidden from you. He wants to guide you.

In The End, Trust God.

Trying to discover your life purpose can be a stressful, overwhelming thing. It can seem like such a big, confusing, frustrating subject. You want to move forward, but you're not sure how. You want to find your purpose, but you feel like you're aimlessly wandering.

But you can trust God to lead you where he wants you to go. As Psalm 23:2-3 says, "He leads me beside still waters. He restores my soul. He leads me in paths of righteousness for his name's sake."

You may feel confused, but God is not.

Repeat after me, I trust you God with my whole heart, and I invite you to lead me in my walking in my purpose. Now, trust God and walk in your purpose.

Cultural Competence

Cultural Competence

Cultural competence encourages us to be mindful and show sensitivity to cross-cultural differences, to adapt to other cultural environments, at times, and to be reflective of cultural influences on one's behaviors and thoughts. Researchers have defined cultural competence in many ways. For example:

- "Shared beliefs, values, and assumptions of a group of people who learn from one another and teach to others that their behaviors, attitudes, and perspectives are the correct ways to think, act, and feel." (Schein, 2010)

- "The ability of individuals and systems to work or respond effectively across cultures in a way that acknowledges and respects the culture of the person or organization being served." (Williams, 2001, p.1).

- "The acquisition and maintenance of culture-specific skills" for very practical reasons (Wilson, Ward, and Fischer, 2013):

  - function effectively within a new cultural context.
  - interact effectively with people from different cultural backgrounds.

In this textbook, cultural competence is being defined as the ability to work effectively with people from different cultural backgrounds.

Cultural competence is comprised of four components or aspects:

- a diplomatic mindset,
- agile cultural learning,
- reasoning about other cultures, and
- a disciplined approach to intercultural interactions.

We go through each of these competency areas in more depth, below. Essentially, cultural competence is a set of skills and knowledge that can help you learn, reason, solve problems, and interact comfortably when you're working with people from different cultures. Cultural competence can be improved through training, education, and experience.

In our increasingly connected world, it's not surprising that we are encountering people from all manner of backgrounds in our workplaces. Whether you are leading a diverse team to develop a new product, treating patients from different walks of life, promoting stability in a conflict zone, or teaching in a multicultural classroom, cultural competence is critical to your success in the professional realm.

Building relationships and working successfully with different others can seem like a major challenge. However, you can enjoy the rewards, while keeping frustration to a minimum.

The key to making them work is cultural competence.

Four broad cultural competency domains that have been used to create successful cross-cultural relationships include:

Diplomatic Mindset

Diplomacy is the art of dealing with people in a thoughtful and effective way. Though it's often talked about in connection with international relationships, diplomacy and tact can be applied to every interaction we have with people from other cultures or social backgrounds.

A diplomatic mindset starts with a focus on what you are trying to accomplish. And recognizing that you need to work with diverse others to meet your goals. It means being aware of your own worldview and realizing that your own background shapes how you see things.

Doing so helps you understand how you are viewed by the person you are interacting with. It also helps you manage your own attitudes toward the other person's culture. Making it easier to find ways to get the job done despite your differences.

Cultural Learning

Professionals who successfully navigate cross-cultural relationships actively learn cultural norms, language and customs in an ongoing fashion. There's far too much to know about people and cultures to think that you can read a book or take a class and be done with it.

Cultural learning does not only take place in preparation for an interaction, it continues afterward as well. The professionals would often seek feedback from natives of their host country after an experience to find out what they got wrong and what they could do better in the future.

Cultural Reasoning

Cultural reasoning helps you make sense of cultural behaviors that initially seem odd. Like a scientist with an unexpected result, treat puzzling behaviors as opportunities to deepen your understanding of the culture. Dig in and figure out why they do what they do.

If you're walking into a situation completely fresh, with no context to draw from, all is not lost. Taking a moment to reflect on the 'why' likely leads you to discover a few possible alternatives. Maybe she was trying to get a read on your personal values to gauge how well you'll work together. Or, maybe he was trying to get a rise out of you, to get a sense of how well you manage conflict.

It may not be possible to figure out a person's real motivation in the moment. However, with practice, you'll find that you can regularly take the point of view of diverse people you're working with. You can more readily consider their beliefs and desires in the moment and use that perspective to work together more effectively.

Once you discover people's beliefs and motives, you're in a better position to spot the differences that cause misunderstandings and conflict. And, you have your hands on the levers to positively influence their perceptions and decisions.

Intercultural Interaction

Showing you've taken the time to learn a custom or bit of language goes a long way to build rapport with someone from a different culture. Yet, it's natural to feel awkward and uncertain, or even silly, and so don't shy away from giving it a try.

Fortunately, there is a natural tendency for people to positively respond to someone's attempts to address language and cultural norms, regardless of their performance level.

For example, using a customary greeting in a person's native tongue will be seen positively even if it hits the limit of your language skills.

The connection begins in the attempt. Mastery happens over time.

One solution seasoned professionals use is to plan their critical intercultural communications in advance. This goes beyond rehearsing that greeting to getting your nuanced talking points down before a difficult negotiation.

Cross-cultural experts draw on deep reserves of discipline to face these situations. They manage their reactions and the impression they make, which often earns them greater respect in the process.

When we make a special effort to understand the people we meet, our lives and our relationships are richer for it.

Cultural competence isn't necessarily a skill that can be mastered, because there are always new people to meet. And they bring new cultures, family histories, and worldviews to the table.

Our goal shouldn't be mastery—it can simply be having a heart that's willing to share our own culture and learn about the culture of others.

Here are a few ideas that will help improve your cultural competence:

1. *Pay attention.*

   In today's technology-driven world, it's easy to overlook pretty much everyone and everything around us. If you want to build relationships with the people around you, disconnect and make eye contact. Smile. Say hello. Act like you care, and when you begin to speak or ask questions, people will believe you actually do care.

2. *Listen.*

How often do we engage in conversation with someone with whom we have nothing in common, or someone with whom we disagree on a big topic? Do we ever think to set aside our own discomfort and try to just listen? One of the best ways to become culturally competent is to ask questions, and then listen carefully with interest, without any attempt to interrupt or persuade. Instead of asking what someone believes about a certain topic, ask them *why* they believe what they do. This is an opportunity to learn more about their beliefs, experiences, and perspective.

3. *Use your imagination.*

It's impossible to fully understand what it's like to walk in the shoes of someone whose life experience is polar opposite of your own, but it's valuable to try. Imagine life the way you've heard them describe it, and it'll go a long way in helping you understand other cultures and worldviews.

4. *Show interest.*

Whether it's dinner, a cooking or language lesson, or a special festival that celebrates their culture, go and learn. Invite them to do the same in your world. You'll both be better for having learned something new, and you'll have fun doing it.

Life is richer when we engage with the people around us, inviting them into our world and learning all we can about theirs. And listening to one another, seeking to truly hear them and understand their perspectives, is a crucial step toward peace.

It is critical to know how to assess our cultural competency and evaluate our own cultural behaviors. But developing cultural competence helps us understand, communicate with, and effectively interact with people across cultures. It gives us the ability to compare different cultures with our own and better understand the differences. Unconsciously, we bring our own cultural frame of interpretation to any situation. This is not to say that culture alone determines how one interprets a situation. One's own unique history and personality also play an important role (Hofstede, 2002).

When you have a greater understanding of other cultures you will be able to interact with people from a wide range of backgrounds and you will increase your abilities to help your clients receive the highest level of support.

Cultural competence encourages the acknowledgement and acceptance of differences in appearance, behavior and culture. In this field, you will encounter diverse clients from a wide range of backgrounds. Even students who come from diverse neighborhoods will likely come in contact with new cultures as they enter the Human Services field. As we develop our levels of cultural competence, we begin to have a greater appreciation for our clients' journeys.

Displaying empathy and compassion by fostering mutual respect between the worker and the client is the foundation of any Human Services practice. As such, cultural competence is an integral component in this process.

Who Am I?
My Beliefs and Values

"Who am I?" gets at the heart of one of our most basic needs: our need for identity.

Our identity is our all-encompassing system of memories, experiences, feelings, thoughts, relationships, and values that define who each of us is. These components we can identify and understand. Then, once we have understood the components of our identity, we can get a big-picture look at who we are.

Identity is a critical component of understanding who we are. Why? Because we can break up identity into components (values, experiences, relationships).

We, as living beings, search for and find comfort in a solid sense of identity. It grounds us. It gives us confidence. And our sense of identity affects every single thing in our lives – from the choices we make to the values we live by.

Yet, our sense of identity can be compromised by outside factors. The more you look for external fixes to sort out your life, the further you be venture from learning how to live your life aligned with a deeper sense of inner purpose.

There are 5 key steps you can take to help answer the question "who am I?"

These steps are backed by experts and will help you firm up your identity so that you can live a life full of purpose.

Here are 5 ways to help answer the question, "who am I?"

1. Reflect

You need to reflect upon yourself whenever you are engaging in self-discovery.

This means that you have to examine yourself — for all your strengths, flaws, impressions you give others, the whole lot. You have to critically engage with the reflection you present.

You have to be your inspector. You have to look at your whole self as the house and get down deep to that foundation.

Ask yourself, who are you right now? What are your strengths? Your flaws? Do you like who you see in the mirror? Do you think that "who you are" doesn't match "who you see?"

How does that make you feel?

Identify which areas of your life you are unhappy about. Look at what you think could be better – mentally, emotionally, and physically.

Don't go rush and slap band-aids all over the issues. This step isn't about quick fixes. It's not even about changing anything. Instead, it's about sitting with yourself — ups and downs — and understanding where you are. Once you have a good grasp on yourself, then you can move on to step two.

2. Decide who you want to be

You can never be a perfect person. There's no such thing as a perfect person. You have to embrace the fact that you will never be perfect. But, on the path to self-discovery, you should embrace that there are things you want to improve. And improvement is possible!

So, for step two, what you need to do is identify who you want to become. And be honest with yourself about what's possible.

Who is your ideal person? Is it someone kind, strong, intelligent, brave? Is it a person who isn't afraid of a challenge? Is it a person who can open herself up to love? Whoever this dream person is, define them. Define who you want to become. That's step two.

3. Make better choices

Make better choices… for yourself.

The truth is, most of us are programmed to make choices out of fear. We instinctively make an easy choice based on anxiety, desire to please, or because we don't want to put in the effort.

These choices only do one thing: continue the status quo.

And if you're not happy with who you are, with your current status quo, then these choices do nothing to help you. Those choices, then, are the bad choices. But you can choose better for yourself. You can make "active decisions."

> *"Choice means you are free to do or not do something because you decided on your own."*
>
> *—Marcia Reynolds*
> *Clinical Psychologist*

To activate conscious choice, you first have to do some work to determine what really matters to you. What strengths are you proud of? What tasks do you most enjoy? What dreams keep haunting you? What would you do if you had no obligations or people to please? Take time to sort through your desires.

Once you know what you want, and once you know who you want to be; you can take the time to make active, conscious choices that help you be better.

Once you make decisions that are in line with your values and what you want, you'll start feeling empowered to find out your true identity.

4. *Explore your passions*

One of the best parts about discovering the answer to "who am I," is figuring out parts of yourself you never knew about. Sure, you've figured out who you "want to be" and you've done a great job "looking in the mirror," but there's always going to be parts of you that are hidden away. And it's your job to discover them.

One of the best ways to help discover yourself is to explore your passions. When you engage in things you are passionate about, you stimulate creative energies. This exploration will give you confidence and expertise, which helps positively ground your sense of identity. But what if I don't know what I'm passionate about.

When your identity has been built by society's expectations, it's natural that you might not know what you're passionate about. That's ok! But if you haven't, don't go looking for it. Instead, develop it.

"Passion is not a job, a sport or a hobby. It is the full force of your attention and energy that you give to whatever is right in front of you. And if you're so busy looking for this passion, you could miss opportunities that change your life."

–Terri Trespicio

Developing a growth mindset is a key component of exploring your passions. Along the way, you'll figure out who you are. If you're looking for some inspiration in developing a growth mindset.

5. *Develop your social circle*

Humans are social beings by nature. So much of our identity is shaped by our friends and family. When you work to figure out "who you are," you have to actively create your social circle. This means choosing who you want to hang out with. It means choosing who to let in, and who to cut loose.

You must find people who are aligned with your values and identity.

When you understand what's most important to you in life – your life values – you can clarify who you are by choosing your social circles based on compatible values. You can have great clarity in your relationships, too, as you see yourself reflected in the people around you.

The task of finding out who you are isn't an easy one. It's probably one of the hardest things you'll ever take on. One of the worst things you can do (during this process) is to put pressure on yourself to figure it out right away. Discovering your identity is a journey, not an ending. Your identity is an ongoing process.

Yes! Our identity should be seen as an ongoing process. Rather than a static snapshot, we should embrace a flowing sense of self, whereby we are perpetually reframing, reorganizing, rethinking, and reconsidering ourselves. How different would life be if rather than asking "Who am I?" we contemplated how we'd like to engage life?

The emphasis shouldn't be on discovering who you *are* (what is buried beneath) but on facilitating the emergence of what you'd like to experience.

Many of us struggle with finding direction, making big decisions, and even knowing how to act in day-to-day situations. When you take the time to consider your core values, these things become crystal clear.

Core values point the needle of your compass, illuminating the pathway toward living a meaningful life — one that's filled with passion and purpose.

It's time to envision a life you're insanely passionate about. A life that would fulfill your wildest dreams. A life that can only be achieved by reassessing your current value system. Then create a custom life plan to achieve it, including your new mission/purpose in life, a list of values and beliefs that help you achieve that mission and give you ways to set new goals for yourself.

Using your values to guide your decisions goes back to understanding what drives you. What causes you to take action? What's the driving force behind your goals? Are you someone who seeks thrill or stability? Do you gravitate toward pleasure or pain? What gets you out of bed in the morning feeling energized and joyful?

By examining these invisible influences, you can redefine the power these forces have over your life. This will help you reset your intentions toward success and joy, instead of misery and suffering, ultimately helping you to live a more fulfilling and successful life. It's up to you to shift your focus to important values and beliefs, because as Tony says, "What you value determines what you focus on."

Your personal values and beliefs deeply affect how you create and maintain healthy relationships. Relationships can be a major source of joy and love, but they can also cause intense disappointment and sadness. Your limiting beliefs about yourself and others are magnified when you enter a relationship, and that means that your values are also magnified. When two partners find themselves debating values vs. beliefs, or when limiting beliefs prevent them from finding real connection, the relationship is unlikely to last.

By now you have a clear vision of your values and beliefs and of what you want your life to look like. You understand that each thought and action in your day are leading you to fulfill your destiny and create an extraordinary life. You know how to control your beliefs instead of letting your beliefs control you. By reevaluating your method for choosing values and decision-making, you'll be armed and ready to create the life you crave.

How to Become a Culturally Competent Coach

Coaching is like improvisation – it is a fluid process that bends and twists and flows in different directions based upon the context and situation.

Developing cultural competence (or CQ = cultural intelligence) is like improvisation. You try one thing based upon your experience, then reflect and regroup, and try another approach.

Displaying the cultural competency behaviors of active listening, empathy, and effective engagement can help us to create a welcoming environment and establish the appreciation of similarities and differences among cultures.

Cultural competence is the ability of a person to effectively interact, work, and develop meaningful relationships with people of various cultural backgrounds. Cultural background can include the beliefs, customs, and behaviors of people from various groups. Gaining cultural competence is a lifelong process of increasing self-awareness, developing social skills and behaviors around diversity, and gaining the ability to advocate for others. It goes beyond tolerance, which implies that one is simply willing to overlook differences. Instead, it includes recognizing and respecting diversity through our words and actions in all contexts.

And just like any skill, the process of development and improvement continues, developing cultural competence is a process rather than an end point. There are many ways by which we can increase our capacity to be effective in our interactions with others.

Fortunately, Janet E. Helms, PhD, Director of the Institute for the Study and Promotion of Race and Culture at Boston College and other experts have given us plenty of ways to get that training and experience on our own:

Learn about yourself.

Get started by exploring your own historical roots, beliefs and values, says Robert C. Weigl, PhD, a psychologist at the Franklin Center in Alexandria, Va., who described a protocol for such self-reflection in a 2009 paper in the *International Journal of Intercultural Relations* (Vol. 33, No. 4). The eight-step process includes such exercises as describing your ancestors and their experiences, thinking about how your family functions as a group, and characterizing your most representative style of thought as emotional or rational, "me-centered" or "we-centered," and the like.

Self-assessment makes participants realize the pervasive role culture plays in their lives, says Weigl. It also makes people aware of their own biases while sparking open-minded curiosity about other cultures. Plus, it's fun, he says, adding that students are "sometimes swept away by healthy narcissism" as they explore their own backgrounds.

Learn about different cultures.

If you know you're going to be researching or providing therapy to people with unfamiliar backgrounds, seek cultural insight through journal articles and academic books. But don't stop there. "There's a richness to memoirs, for example, that scientific journal articles just cannot capture. Try reading novels such as "The God of Small Things" — an examination of India's caste system — and such documentaries as "Divided We Fall," about post-9-11 hate crimes against South Asians.

However, one of the best ways to immerse yourself in another culture's worldview is to learn a second language, says private practitioner Pamela A. Hays, PhD, of Soldotna, Alaska, and author of "Addressing Cultural Complexities in Practice: Assessment, Diagnosis, and Therapy" (APA, 2008). "One of the most mind-expanding experiences is to learn a word or concept that doesn't exist in your own language," she says. "Plus, learning a language means you're more able to reach out and connect with people who speak that language."

Interact with diverse groups.

Arranging a research project, practicum experience or internship where you work with people from a culture that's unfamiliar to you is a great way to enhance your cultural competence. Depending on the kinds of cultural experiences you're seeking, you may want to volunteer at community centers, religious institutions or soup kitchens. Take a friend or two with you and spend some time afterward discussing how the experience may have changed your views.

It's also important to supplement work and volunteer experience with nonclinical social interactions, recommends Hays. Instead of solely interacting with members of diverse groups who are seeking help, get a fuller picture by interacting with them as peers at parties, religious services and cultural events. "Put yourself in social situations where you're the only one of your cultural group," she recommends.

Attend diversity-focused conferences.

Get formal training on diversity-related research and practice issues, learn about the latest research, and meet potential collaborators at APA's Annual Convention, as well as conferences that are focused specifically on diversity issues.

Lobby your department.

If your program isn't giving you the training you need, push the faculty to do better, says Helms. Whether you plan to send the departmental chair a formal letter with concrete suggestions and complaints or handle the matter more informally, be sure to gather allies — students from within and outside your department — to help you make your case. That way, says Helms, "the program gets the message that this is something important to students."

And remember: These steps are just the beginning, says Hays.

"Cultural competence is a lifelong project," she says, adding that competence with one group doesn't mean you're competent with another. "You have to keep finding ways to expand your learning."

With these skills, coaches are uniquely equipped to help multi-cultural teams practice curiosity and open questioning. Active listening and humility are essential for coaches looking to partner with clients from another culture. Asking the client how their values come from their experiences and culture puts their needs at the center of the coaching conversation. An adaptive coach also reflects on how their own experiences and culture contribute to personal bias. Individuals are rarely a perfect representation of a single culture and often have overlapping identities that guide their actions.

Because when a coach understands an individual's relationship to a structure, belief system, or set of experiences, they can better guide that person to make sustained change in line with their identity and values. Other cultures may highlight productivity, personal insight, or respect for hierarchy as top priorities. Beyond an individual's internal reality, adaptive coaches must understand the interpersonal relationships of their clients and how they interact with their family, community, or society.

Culturally competent coaching is about partnering with clients to create their own standards for success. In a globally connected world, coaches who understand how culture shapes both their clients' and their own experiences can strengthen collaboration and elevate diverse voices in decision-making. Coaches are uniquely equipped to guide individuals, organizations, communities, and policymakers to reduce inequalities through mutual understanding.

Evidenced Based

Life Coaching and Positive Psychology

Positive psychology has a big influence on the field of coaching.

But wondering how life coaching and positive psychology are connected? Let's start with some simple definitions to get clear about the differences, and where these two disciplines intersect.

What's Life Coaching?

Life coaching is a partnership where a coach and client come together to accomplish a specific and measurable goal. Rather than telling the client "how to get there," coaching holds that each person carries innate wisdom, and is capable of developing their own answers.

As coaches, we assist this process by helping our clients think strategically, identify self-imposed limitations, and overcome roadblocks.

What's Positive Psychology?

Positive psychology is the science behind how individuals and groups flourish and thrive. It's the study of emotions, behaviors and beliefs that emphasize human strengths rather than weaknesses.

Positive psychology provides new empirical data and specific tools to help people move along a continuum from "baseline wellness" to a state of thriving.

Why Positive Psychology Matters in Life Coaching

The value of coaching is ultimately determined by the outcomes our clients achieve. There are times, though, when clients don't themselves know how to articulate the outcome they're really looking for. People often hire a life coach because they believe they need help overcoming an area of weakness. They may think the key to achieving their goals is simply a matter of discipline and accountability.

Underneath the stated goal a client comes to coaching with, there may be an even more fundamental desire that has not been expressed. The desire to feel content. To be happy. To feel more satisfied with themselves, and their life.

What many people don't realize is that psychologists don't just provide counseling and therapy for mental health issues such as anxiety, depression, post traumatic stress, etc.

Psychologists can also help you to become more effective in any – or all - areas of your life: work/life balance, career, relationships, family, health and wellbeing, leadership, or finances.

Research has shown that not only are physical, mental, and social well-being important components for complete health, but they are also interconnected. Evidence is accumulating that a happy, engaged, and fulfilling psychological and social life is not just a consequence of good health, it is what leads people to live a healthy and long life.

In addition, the importance of social support and positive relationships on good health and well-being has long been documented. Supportive social relationships were associated with longevity, less cognitive decline with aging, greater resistance to infectious disease, and better management of chronic illnesses.

And we suspect that positive psychology interventions, when successful, lead people not only to think and feel in more positive ways but also to behave in more healthy ways. Intervention studies allow us to conclude that interventions informed by positive psychology can indeed change positive psychological states and traits, sometimes in lasting ways. An important qualification is that long-term benefits do not result from one-shot interventions unless these lead to a change in how someone habitually lives.

All of these factors may lead to healthier behaviors and habits and eventually to better health.

Researchers have shown that positive psychology interventions influence some of the biological and behavioral processes implicated in good health (Nansook, Peterson, Szvarca, & Vander Molen, Kim, & Collon, 2014).

In short, positive psychology is the scientific study of the strengths and virtues that enable individuals and communities to thrive. It is a rich and growing field and aligns perfectly with coaching: both assume people are basically healthy, resourceful, and motivated to grow.

What are the Benefits of Positive Psychology Coaching?

Research (Nansook, et al., 2014) has demonstrated that a number of positive psychology practices can effectively raise our level of happiness. The benefits of happiness are significant and widespread and extend far beyond just feeling good.

Happier people tend to enjoy better health, live a longer life, have closer friendships, are more creative and productive at work and in life, and achieve greater success.

Research studies show that the happiest people tend to:

- Express gratitude—that is, counting their blessings
- Nurture relationships with family and friends
- Practice optimism regarding the future
- Savor the positive experience in their lives
- Commit to and realize meaningful goals

Positive psychology is a natural fit with coaching. Clients seek out coaching for a full range of issues, but underneath all of these issues is a generally unstated desire to increase their overall sense of happiness and well-being.

Positive emotions prepare us for growth by broadening our mindset. The more moments we experience inside a broadened mindset, the more we can fundamentally change who we are and become better versions of ourselves. As coaches, THIS is the state of mind we want to help our clients cultivate!

How does Positive Psychology Help Coaches?

Today, Positive Psychology offers us a scientific approach for understanding human potential, along with a set of research-based interventions and practices for achieving it. And the primary aim is to help us develop an inner toolkit for growth and life satisfaction that's rooted in our personal strengths.

By providing evidence-based tools that can help drive lasting change and increase overall satisfaction in life. For life coaches who want a framework for helping their clients get consistent and measurable results, there are many effective interventions to draw from.

Positive psychology techniques coaches frequently use include:

- Knowing and appreciating your strengths
- Identifying personal values and priorities
- Understanding your life purpose
- Cultivating positive emotions and gratitude
- Resilience and coping skills
- Reframing a situation to recognize where you have agency, ability, and tools to make change
- Self-acceptance and compassion
- Future visioning and working toward a "best possible future self"
- Developing healthy habits and strengthening personal accountability

These evidence-based tools drawn from the field of positive psychology can help you make a greater impact in your life coaching practice.

Life Coaching and Cognitive Behavioral Coaching

Cognitive Behavioral Coaching (CBC) is a powerful coaching model that draws on evidence based psychological models such as Cognitive Behavioral Therapy (Lungu, et al., 2021). The strategies, activities, techniques, and exercises used are effective in helping individuals identify and challenge self-defeating thoughts, feelings, and behaviors. Negative thinking leads to negative emotions and negative emotions lead to negative behaviors, all of which influences an individual's physiology.

Many common daily challenges such as stress, lack of confidence, perfectionism, loss of meaning and purpose, poor communication skills or being less successful at work usually lead back to an individual's personal perception of self.

The aim of Cognitive Behavioral Coaching or CBC as it is known, is to develop ways of thinking and associated behaviors that are more productive and likely to assist an individual reach their desired goals in life. The process helps clients move towards becoming the kind of person they want to be, attaining desired outcomes whether personal or professional.

It also aims to help clients gain a perspective about whatever is at the root of that person's difficulty. Coach and client work collaboratively to identify what might be stopping an individual from reaching his or her full potential and what action is needed to take charge of their situation.

Coaching has emerged as a new intervention that applies behavioral science to help clients improve their well-being and performance. It assists clients in reaching desired goals by focusing on growth, values, meaning, self-awareness, and self-actualization. At the same time, coaching poses several challenges.

Coaches also need to have growth mindsets to view their clients as experts on their personal experience and be open to modifying methods and techniques as they arm themselves with new information (Lungu, et al., 2021).

On the other hand, people with growth mindsets have beliefs that can change with more information, critical thought, and commitment. Clients and patients need to adopt growth mindsets to imagine the possibility of change in their lives and improve their subjective well-being.

It is possible to develop a growth mindset in health either in yourself or in your client. Some of the ways to do this include (Lungu, et al., 2021):

- Acknowledging and embracing imperfections
- Viewing challenges as opportunities
- Trying new and diverse ways of achieving the same goal
- Informing yourself with the latest research and guidelines around health conditions and chronic illness prevention
- Valuing the process over the result
- Celebrating growth with others
- Rewarding actions rather than traits
- Emphasizing growth over speed
- Recognizing improvements even when the goals haven't been reached
- Placing effort before talent
- Learning from mistakes
- Making new goals for every goal achieved

Health professionals are often thinking about their clients' mindsets and how these influence their clients' health journeys. However, as the coach, your mindset is of primary importance before thinking about the potential influence you can have on your clients. Your clients' way of looking at their health and well-being will be significantly influenced by your mindset and understanding of everything from what influences health behavior to the "ideal" behaviors to adopt.

One important thing to keep in mind is that coaches are seen as experts and teachers by their clients. They believe that their coaches know how to evaluate a person's health status and that they are experts on how to support their clients in achieving realistic lifestyle modifications.

In other words, coaches' mindsets will have an impact on their clients' mindset. A coach's position is ultimately one of power but also of responsibility.

Thus, coaches must continue to educate themselves and gain sensitivity to the complex factors that influence health behaviors, including environmental and social aspects.

However, health behavior change theories are limited in offering concrete tools for helping coaches work with clients to *adopt actions* that support their long-term health while still being sensitive to experiential differences, like those related to race, culture, trauma, discrimination, socioeconomic status, gender, and others.

To understand health behavior change, you must understand what constitutes a health behavior.

Experts define health behaviors as actions or activities that individuals undertake to maintain or improve their health, prevent health issues, slow disease progression or regression, or achieve what they perceive as a positive body image.

Health behaviors are not entirely individual choices. They are influenced by social determinants, like ideologies, discrimination, inequalities, and agency; environmental determinants, like access to safe sidewalks and a variety of low-cost food; and psychological determinants, like anxiety, depression, eating disorders, and addictions.

Some health outcomes may be easily measurable, like weight gain or weight loss and triglyceride or cholesterol levels. Other outcomes, like motivation and a sense of well-being, may be more challenging to measure but are equally important.

Health professionals are often thinking about their clients' mindsets and how these influence their clients' health journeys. However, as the coach, your mindset is of primary importance before thinking about the potential influence you can have on your clients. Your clients' way of looking at their health and well-being will be significantly influenced by your mindset and understanding of everything from what influences health behavior to the "ideal" behaviors to adopt.

In many ways, supporting your clients to adopt healthy lifestyles through health behaviors is at the core of health coaching. By nature, coaches step away from one-size-fits-all solutions and listen to clients' unique challenges and goals to support them in making realistic shifts in the choices they make. The goal is to improve health outcomes, whether it be as measurable as lower cholesterol levels or as holistic as increasing a sense of well-being.

As health coaches, you explore research-supported methods for approaching problems and evaluate whether they can be applied within the collaborative plan you have built with your client.

In the most basic sense, empathy involves the human ability to understand a person's feelings and perspectives and why they may carry out specific actions. The first step in the healthcare environment, including health coaching, is to put people first to make an effort to truly understand why a person thinks, makes decisions, and takes actions that affect their health as they do.

Change Your Mindset, Change Your Life!

—Dr. Carletta N. Artis

Life Coaching and Attachment Theory

The aim of attachment theory has largely been to explain how relationships with parents and other caregivers in childhood have such a persistent effect on personality development. The focus of attachment theory has subsequently been extended from child to adolescent and adult development and social relationships within the context of both contemporary personality and social psychology. Attachment has been viewed as a natural phenomenon sought by all human beings.

Subsequently, attachment theory postulates that, whereas successful bids for proximity and connectedness with warm, kind, dependable, and encouraging attachment figures are important for optimal functioning, the loss of such proximity and connection can be a natural source of distress and psychosocial dysfunction.

Given that coaching is an interpersonal affair, it is important that both coach and client have an appreciation for the potential impact that their attachment styles can have on their own and the other's behaviors, thoughts, and feelings. As described earlier, an avoidant attachment style is reflected in an individual's being heavily self-reliant and uninterested and unwilling to connect with others.

Ultimately, coaches' persistent positive interpersonal behaviors are more likely to help them satisfy basic psychological needs and promote their well-being.

The role of attachment is crucial in human functioning and affects the way we interact and work with others. Humans are relational beings who require interaction, stimulation and contact with others. The term attachment relates to how we seek closeness or intimacy with others. This includes the relationships we form and maintain with family members, friends and partners. An attachment is not simply a connection between two people, but a deep and meaningful bond that involves the desire for regular contact with that other person, and a sense of distress during a separation.

How Attachments Form

The formation of attachments begins in the first few years of an infant's life when they rely on their parents or caregivers to provide them with love and care and to protect them from harm in the world. Infants rely on their parents or caregivers to provide them with both their emotional and physical needs. When the infant has a need, they may express this through crying. In an ideal situation the parent or caregiver recognizes these needs and satisfies the need through attending to the infant.

It is within these interactions throughout the infant's development that the infant is able form an attachment with their parent or caregiver. In this attachment they learn that the world is a safe place, and ideally form a secure base from which to explore the world. This attachment process is reciprocal, and the bond formed between caregiver and infant is one of deep nurturing.

Attachment Styles in Adults

Through attachments, infants learn to love, care and trust others as they grow up and become adults. The experience of early attachments informs their abilities to regulate their emotions and to become aware of other people's thoughts and feelings. The formation of secure attachments is crucial, but when the needs of an infant are not appropriately met and they are not given the chance to develop the trusting, meaningful bond with parent or caregiver that is so vital, an insecure attachment can be developed and sustained into adult life.

Below I have listed both secure and insecure adult attachment styles.

Secure

Individuals with a secure attachment style were fortunate enough to have had parents or caregivers who were consistently responsive to their needs and enabled them to have a sense that they can be self reliant and also reach out to others when necessary. They can confidently seek fulfillment in their lives and are more likely to be able to manage stress and difficulty. These individuals tend to have positive relationships with others and are more able to manage care, love and experience nurturing relationships. They will be more able to feel comfortable with both intimacy and independence.

Insecure / Anxious-preoccupied

Individuals with anxious-preoccupied attachments will tend to desire emotionally intimate contact with others but find that others may often be reluctant to be as intimate as they would like. They may be uncomfortable without close relationships, but also worry they value others much more than others value them. They will often seek high levels of intimacy, approval and responsiveness from others. They will tend to value intimacy so much that they become overly dependent in their partners. Anxious-preoccupied individuals tend to have fewer positive views about themselves and feel a sense of anxiety which may only lessen when in contact with their partner. Often, they will doubt their worth as a partner and may blame themselves when their partner or friend is not responsive to their needs.

Dismissive-avoidant

Individuals who have a dismissive-avoidant attachment style are more likely to be emotionally removed, distant or disengaged. They can have a tendency to believe that their needs are probably not going to be met by the people in their lives. These individuals can sense that they are slightly withdrawn from others and are not comfortable within relationships. These individuals are also more likely to remain in situations that they find comfortable, and safe, not situations which are new or potentially difficult. In their younger years, these individuals had parents who were disengaged from them. They may have been left to cry for extended periods of time as a baby, which may have been done with the intention of fostering independence. The child then learns that their needs are unlikely to be met, and therefore for self-protection they withdraw and stop reaching out.

Fearful-avoidant

Individuals who develop a fearful-avoidant attachment style may in their past have experienced losses or trauma, such as sexual abuse in childhood or adolescence. They will have mixed feelings about intimate relationships. On the one hand, they desire to be close to another person but on the other, they find emotional closeness difficult and uncomfortable They will find it difficult to trust others, or completely depend upon them and may at times worry that they will be hurt, if they allow themselves to become close to another person.

Often fearful-avoidant individuals will have a set of negative emotions and feelings about themselves and tend to view themselves as unworthy of responsiveness from their partners. Due to this, they will find it difficult to seek intimacy from others, not trust the true intentions of their partner and will be less able to express their affection.

Often, adult attachment styles may not be directly visible on the surface, and it may be that you are questioning why relationships are breaking down, or why you are finding it difficult to form trust with others. Therapy can provide you with a safe and non-judgmental space to explore your attachments in adult life, think about your past relationships and develop a greater sense of any relational patterns which may be occurring in your adult life. It will also enable you to develop ways of becoming more secure in your relationships and allow you to feel more able to develop relationships in the future.

So how do we develop this feeling of having a secure base, or safe haven if it is not in our systems from our childhood? How can we change this for our future children and grandchildren? This change from one type of attachment to another does not happen overnight, it is a process. One of the ways to start is to work on moving to a secure attachment type, which takes having a secure base and a "safe haven person." This person's role is to be consistently attuned during sessions and to help develop trust. With an attuned coach or therapist, one can work through their old wounds and issues. The coach or therapist plays the role of the parent (or original primary caregiver). Therefore, it is an authority role, not a love relationship role as peers.

We are born with the need to be taken care, touched, and held for our brains and nervous systems to hook up properly. We are products of our parents before us and their parents before them. It is like a giant wave, and we are a ripple in the current. Why would we think that just because we are now adults that we need to do this alone, if we have the wounding of insecurity? We need to develop a relationship with another person that becomes our so-called, "parent" to work though these issues, to heal them. Then, when we learn to really trust in life, we become a secure attachment person.

Despite individuals saying they do not trust anyone, we must trust, and we do trust. It is not simply a matter of to trust or not to trust, it is more of who cannot trust and who you can trust, and what you can trust them with. For example, in love relationships, we trust the other person to be faithful, to be a financial support, to be an emotional support, to even take out the garbage on Thursdays. So, you can do it. In fact, you are doing it. You can trust. Everyone needs someone to trust and rely on, even if it's not perfect. None of us are perfect and none of us get it right 100% of the time. Think about it.

Skills Training

Communication Skills

Communication skills enable individuals to understand others and to be understood themselves. A variety of aspects are important in the context of these skills, such as listening, speaking, observing and empathy.

In everyday life, these skills are required to communicate ideas to others, develop a confident attitude, respect for others and public speaking. Developing these skills helps many people make progress in the workplace.

Effective communication consists of both speaking and listening. Active listening is a way of listening and responding to another person that improves mutual understanding. It is an important first step to defuse the situation and seek solutions to problems.

Like critical thinking and problem-solving skills, active listening is a soft skill that's held in high regard by employers. When interviewing for jobs, using active listening techniques can show the interviewer how your interpersonal skills can draw people out.

It involves paying attention to the conversation, not interrupting, and taking the time to understand what the speaker is discussing. The "active" element involves taking steps to draw out details that might not otherwise be shared. Or the process by which an individual secures information from another individual or group. And a helpful skill for any worker to develop. It helps you truly understand what people are saying in conversations and meetings (and not just what you *want* to hear, or *think* you hear).

This helps you to make other people feel heard and valued. We can name active listening skills as the foundation for any successful conversation. It uses verbal and non-verbal techniques.

Verbal Active Listening Techniques

1. *Paraphrase* – summarizing the message the speaker shared will allow the speaker to clarify the information or expand their message it will also help you to fully understand their meaning.

2. *ASK open-ended Questions* – these questions show that you have gathered the essence of what they've shared and can guide them in sharing more information with you. These questions should not be answered with a simple yes, or no. For example –"you're right- the onboarding needs some updating. What are the changes you would like to make to this process over the next six months"?

3. *Ask specific probing questions* – these are often called direct questions.it guides the reader so that he/she can provide more details about the information that they have shared. Example- "Tell me about your workload. Which of these projects are more time-consuming?"

4. *Using short verbal affirmations* – is used to make the speaker feel more comfortable and show that you're engaged and can process the information that he is delivering. These affirmations are Short and positive. This will help you to continue the conversation without interrupting or disrupting their flow. Example – "I Understand.", "I agree", "OH! I See ", etc.

5. *Displaying empathy* – showing compassion rather than just feeling it will connect you with the speaker and will help you in establishing a sense of mutual trust. Make sure that the speaker can understand that you're able to recognize their emotions and share their feelings. Example -"I am sorry you're dealing with this problem, let's figure out some ways I can help."

6. *Share similar Experiences* – this will show the speaker that you have successfully interpreted their message. This can also help you in building relationships. For example – The speaker has shared with you the XYZ problem and you provided input on how to solve a similar problem you were facing

7. *Recalling previously shared information* – try to remember the important points, concepts, and ideas that the speaker has shared with you in the past. This will make the speaker understand that you are not only listening but are also able to retain the information and recall the specific details.

Non-Verbal Active Listening Skills

1. *Nods* – during the conversation a few simple nods will show the speaker that you understand what they are saying and encourage them to share the information further. This shows that you can process the meaning of their message.

2. *Smile* – like a nod, smile also encourages the speaker to continue. This can often signify that you are happy about what they have to say. In some cases, it can be assumed that you agree with their message or thought. This can also take place in short verbal affirmation so that the speaker feels comfortable.

3. *Avoid distracting Movements* – you can do this by trying to avoid movements like glancing at the watch or the cell phone, doodling, or tapping a pen. Try to avoid an exchange of verbal and non-verbal communication as this will make the speaker feel frustrated and uncomfortable.

4. *Maintain eye contact* – try to avoid looking at objects and other people in the room. Keep an eye on the speaker just be sure that you don't stare and keep the gaze natural, using nods and a smile to ensure you are encouraging them rather than making them uncomfortable or uneasy.

By following these verbal and non-verbal techniques you can develop strong relationships and retain more information. Although Active listening can only be developed by practicing the techniques. The more likely you are trying to use these techniques the more natural they will feel. Active listening has the purpose of earning the trust of others and understanding their situation and perspective.

As we know, active listening is an important skill. Let's look at some benefits of active listening.

Benefits of Active Listening

1. *Relationships* – Active listening has many benefits in a relationship. It allows you to understand other people and respond to them with empathy. Also, it lets you ask questions to make sure that you understand what is being said. Moreover, it

will make the speaker speak longer where the conversation is more about your partner than about you.

In case your partner is going through a tough time it will be helpful and valuable to your partner and the relationship. Here the goal won't be to be heard and to solve only your problem, so it is less likely to jump in a "quick fix".

2. *Social situations* – Active listening will help you to meet new people and learn more about them by asking questions, seeking clarification, and watching body language. The newly met people can turn into friends as when you listen actively the other person is also likely to speak to you for a longer time.

3. *Work* – active listening plays an important role if you are in a supervisory position, or you want to interact with colleagues or clients.it will help you to understand the collaboration to develop solutions. This also reflects your patience. it helps you build connections as active listening will make the other person comfortable with you and share information with you.

When you sincerely listen to what others say they will also be interested in communicating with you on a regular basis this will lead to the opening of opportunities. It also helps you to increase your knowledge and understand various topics and also helps you to avoid missing critical information when you can speak.

Because most times when we hear things, we are engaged in passive listening—we expect our brains to capture the main points and remember them for later. However, active listening is an important skill when it comes to good communication. Becoming a better listener takes practice, but it will improve your ability to connect with other people and increase your capacity to retain information.

Active Listening is an important part of your communication skill set because it encourages openness, honesty, and success. When you pay attention to your conversation partner, you show that person they are being heard, thus building trust and making that person feel like their words matter to you.

Cognitive Therapy Skills

Cognitive is a technical word used to describe anything related to thoughts. In this chapter, we explore how it is that our thoughts can lead to negative emotions, and what we can do about it.

Cognitive Therapy Skills (Hoffman, et al., 2012) involve responding to and modifying our thoughts—to help us cope better in our daily lives and feel less anxious.

How do Cognitive Therapy Skills Work?

The main goal of cognitive skills is to gather evidence. Like a detective, we look to uncover facts about something that has happened in the past or is happening right now.

By examining our thoughts, beliefs, and basic assumptions in detail, we can learn to make informed choices about issues that impact us. For example, we may find that a thought is not completely true; this helps us decrease our efforts to protect ourselves and lowers our anxiety. Another option is to take these facts and do something with them– to problem solve. Finally, these facts may help us understand that nothing can be done to change a situation; we work to accept this and let go of our efforts to control. In order to choose one of these options we use cognitive skills to understand thoughts and situations as well as possible.

Cognitive Therapy Skills are one set of skills used in CBT. They are based on the idea that our thoughts can affect how we feel.

What is (CBT) Cognitive Behavioral Therapy?

Cognitive behavioral therapy (CBT) is a type of psychotherapeutic treatment that helps people learn how to identify and change destructive or disturbing thought patterns that have a negative influence on behavior and emotions (Early, 2016).

Cognitive behavioral therapy focuses on changing the automatic negative thoughts that can contribute to and worsen emotional difficulties, depression, and anxiety (Early, 2016). These spontaneous negative thoughts have a detrimental influence on mood. Through CBT, these thoughts are identified, challenged, and replaced with more objective, realistic thoughts.

Cognitive skills are best used in combination with behavioral skills. If we can understand how dangerous a situation is, we can make good decisions about whether it would improve our lives if we were to stop avoiding a situation or over-protecting ourselves, which can be limiting.

While each type of cognitive behavioral technique takes a different approach, all work to address the underlying thought patterns that contribute to psychological distress.

CBT Techniques and Skills

CBT is about more than identifying thought patterns; it is focused on using a wide range of strategies to help people overcome these thoughts. Techniques may include journaling, role-playing, relaxation techniques, and mental distractions. Here are more techniques in detail.

Identifying Negative Thoughts

It is important to learn how thoughts, feelings, and situations can contribute to maladaptive behaviors.[5] The process can be difficult, especially for people who struggle with introspection, but it can ultimately lead to self-discovery and insights that are an essential part of the treatment process.

Practicing New Skills

It is important to start practicing new skills that can then be put in to use in real-world situations. For example, a person with a substance use disorder might start practicing new coping skills and rehearsing ways to avoid or deal with social situations that could potentially trigger a relapse.

Goal-Setting

Goal setting can an important step in recovery from mental illness and helping you make changes to improve your health and life. During CBT, a therapist can help with goal-setting skills by teaching you how to identify your goal, distinguish between short- and long-term goals, set SMART (specific, measurable, attainable, relevant, time-based) goals, and focus on the process as much as the end outcome.

Problem-Solving

Learning problem solving skills can help you identify and solve problems that arise from life stressors, both big and small, and reduce the negative impact of psychological and physical illness.

- Problem solving in CBT often involves five steps:
- Identifying a problem
- Generating a list of possible solutions
- Evaluating the strengths and weaknesses of each possible solution
- Choosing a solution to implement
- Implementing the solution

Self-Monitoring

Also known as diary work, self-monitoring is an important part of CBT that involves tracking behaviors, symptoms, or experiences over time and sharing them with your therapist. Self-monitoring can help provide your therapist with the information needed to provide the best treatment. For example, for people coping with eating disorders, self-monitoring may involve keeping track of eating habits as well as any thoughts or feelings that went along with consuming that meal or snack.

CBT is based on the idea that how we think (cognition), how we feel (emotion) and how we act (behavior) all interact together. Specifically, our thoughts determine our feelings and our behavior.

Therefore, negative and unrealistic thoughts can cause us distress and result in problems. When a person suffers with psychological distress, the way in which they interpret situations becomes skewed, which in turn has a negative impact on the actions they take.

CBT aims to help people become aware of when they make negative interpretations, and of behavioral patterns which reinforce the distorted thinking. Cognitive therapy helps people to develop alternative ways of thinking and behaving which aims to reduce their psychological distress.

Negative automatic thoughts are negative thoughts that come automatically to us when we are feeling anxious, depressed, angry, frustrated; they can come any time we have a negative emotion. We all have them. Sometimes they pop into our heads uninvited. Sometimes they stick in our heads for hours.

When we are anxious, the brain wants us to think about potentially dangerous things in our environment, in order to keep us safe. We want our anxiety radar to be sensitive if there is actual danger out there.[38]

Maybe it's an overly judgmental inner voice that constantly points out past mistakes and perceived faults. Or maybe it's perpetual worry about the future and comparison to other people.

For many of us, negative thinking patterns are the source of tremendous emotional suffering and misery. In fact, they're the key drivers of both depression and anxiety.

And while negative thinking can feel completely automatic and outside our control, with the right practice and techniques, you can learn how to re-train your mind's habitual way of thinking and free yourself from the burden of negative self-talk.

Cognitive Restructuring is a simple but powerful technique for identifying and undoing negative thinking patterns like worry and rumination.

Why Cognitive Restructuring works?

Let's take a look at how Cognitive Restructuring works by encouraging us to do several very helpful things when we're upset and trying to break free from negative thinking patterns (Hoffman, et al., 2012):

- It helps us get organized mentally. Just like making a to-do list helps us feel more organized and less overwhelmed when we're working on a big project, Cognitive Restructuring helps us feel better by getting our mental space better organized.

- It forces us to slow down. Every negative thought leads to a corresponding "dose" of negative emotion. If you can slow down your thinking and have fewer thoughts, you'll end up with less emotion.

- It helps us be more aware. Thoughts and the emotional reactions they produce can happen quite automatically. Cognitive Restructuring helps us notice and become more aware of our mental habits, which is an essential step in eventually modifying them.

- It gives us a sense of agency and control. By noticing our default thinking patterns as just that, a default, and then generating new alternative thoughts, we change negative thoughts from something uncontrollable that happens to us to things we actually have a good amount of control over.

- It helps us think more clearly and rationally. By encouraging us to question and examine our initial line of thinking, Cognitive Restructuring helps us to see errors or mistakes in the way we're thinking. As we'll see in a later section, identifying Cognitive Distortions is a key ingredient in managing our negative thinking patterns and moods better.

- It helps us reflect instead of reacting. When we're upset, it's natural to just react—worry more, crack open another beer, distract ourselves with YouTube, etc. Aside from the negative effects that go along with some of our favorite reactions to being upset ("empty" calories, wasted time, etc.), by always reacting without reflecting, we deprive ourselves of the opportunity to better understand our minds and learn how they work. Which of course is important if we want them to run more smoothly.

- It breaks bad mental habits. We can get into mental habits (like worry, for example) just as easily as we can get into physical habits like twirling our hair or biting our lip. The key to breaking those habits is to notice when we start doing them and substitute a different behavior. Cognitive Restructuring does just that: it forces us to notice bad mental habits and replace them with better ones.

Cognitive Restructuring is an effective way to identify when we're engaging in the habit of worry and to disengage from it by calling out the irrationality of it and substituting more realistic thought patterns instead. These are just some of the mental skills that Cognitive Restructuring helps us to build.

Never underestimate the power of your thoughts!
You have power.
You have the power to change your thoughts.

−Dr. Carletta N. Artis

Behavior Therapy Skills

Behavioral therapy, or behavior therapy, is a branch of therapy that focuses on teaching individuals to modify harmful, antisocial, or maladaptive behaviors and replace them with positive behaviors, with the ultimate goal of helping the patient navigate life with a greater degree of success and independence.

Types of behavioral therapy

There are a number of different types of behavioral therapy.

Cognitive Behavioral Therapy

Cognitive Behavioral Therapy is extremely popular. It combines behavioral therapy, which focuses on patterns of action, with cognitive therapy, which focuses on patterns of thought.

Treatment is centered around how your thoughts and beliefs influence your actions and moods. It often focuses on your current problems and how to solve them. The long-term goal is to build thinking and behavioral patterns that help you achieve a better quality of life.

Cognitive Behavioral Play Therapy

Cognitive Behavioral Play Therapy is commonly used as a treatment for mental health conditions in children (Knell, 2016). By watching a child play, a therapist is able to gain insight into what a child is uncomfortable expressing or unable to express.

Children may be able to choose their own toys and play freely. They might be asked to draw a picture or use toys to create scenes in a sandbox. Therapists may teach parents how to use play to improve communication with their children.

In this form of play therapy, the therapist also takes a more direct approach by working with both the child and the caregivers to teach the child how to cope well and achieve their defined goals. The therapist is doing more than just watching the child play.

Acceptance And Commitment Therapy (ACT)

ACT is a type of psychotherapy that includes behavioral analysis performed by a mental health clinician. While sometimes compared with CBT, ACT has its own specific approach. ACT is based on relational frame theory, which focuses on mental processes and human language.

In ACT, people are taught mindfulness skills and acceptance strategies with the goal of increasing psychological flexibility. Additionally, commitment and behavior change methods are used.

Dialectical Behavioral Therapy (DBT)

DBT was created by Dr. Marsha Linehan to help treat the symptoms of Borderline Personality Disorder (BPD), an emotional regulation disorder marked by suicidal behavior, depression, unstable personal relationships, and other symptoms (Tolin, 2016).

DBT can also be helpful for conditions other than BPD.

DBT consists of four elements, known as modules:

- core mindfulness
- interpersonal effectiveness, which is used to improve relationships with others and yourself
- emotional regulation
- distress tolerance
- People receiving DBT are taught skills and coping strategies to help them lead healthier, happier lives.

Cognitive Behavioral Coaching Skills

Now let's explore examples of skills created specifically for use in the coaching profession provided by Lungu and colleagues (2021):

SKILLS	DEFINITION
Values	Identifying qualities of ongoing action that bring meaning and vitality to one's life.
Mindful Awareness	Turning attention to the present in a deliberate nonjudgmental way to observe the ongoing stream of thoughts and feelings as they arise.
Cognitive Reappraisal	Identifying ineffective patterns of thinking (i.e., cognitive distortions such as catastrophizing and "should statements"), examining the evidence to support them, and generating more fact-based responses.
Cognitive Defusion	Noticing thinking as it occurs and undermining the impact of thoughts to organize behavior when doing so is not useful.
Acceptance	Adopting a willing and receptive stance toward thoughts and feelings, as well as the circumstances that give rise to them. Foregoing unnecessary or ineffective attempts at suppression and control of internal experience.
Opposite action	Acting in opposition to an urge associated with an emotion (e.g., the desire to withdraw associated with sadness) to reduce the intensity of the emotion and/or choose behavior that is more effective for one's goals.
Distress Tolerance	Strategically distracting oneself from intense emotions when the situations that evoke them are not immediately changeable.
Effective Communication	Expressing oneself in ways that are effective for one's goals in relationships.

Who can Benefit from Behavioral Change?

Behavioral change can benefit people with a wide range of concerns from coaching goals such as career, relationship, and self-improvement to mental health concerns.

People most commonly look for behavioral therapy to treat:

- depression
- anxiety
- panic disorders
- disorders involving excessive anger, like intermittent explosive disorder
  It can also help treat conditions and disorders like:
- eating disorders
- post-traumatic stress disorder
- bipolar disorder
- attention deficit hyperactivity disorder (ADHD)
- phobias, including social phobias
- obsessive compulsive disorder
- self-harming behavior, like cutting
- substance use disorders

Behavior change is recognized by politicians, scientists, and therapists world-wide as crucial to solving individual and social problems. And making changes from existing unhealthy behaviors to new and positive ones is never easy. It takes resources, support, self-determination and self-motivation.

As a result, many behavioral theories have been developed that offer insight into contextual, environmental, individual, and social factors that influence intervention effects and highlight the potential to resolve problems rooted in how we behave.

Creating Good Habits

While goals are crucial to getting things done, sustained change often requires a new set of habits (Clear, 2018).

Clear (2018) states that in order to turn behavior into a habit, it must be:

- Obvious
- Attractive
- Easy
- Satisfying

Undoing Bad Habits

Stopping harmful, negative, or unhelpful habits typically involves preventing their activation in memory or the enactment of the habit response.

Motivation to Change

Motivation is a key factor in initiating and perpetuating change and is a factor in overcoming both resistance and apathy.

Consider the change. Is it the right thing to do? Is it the right time, meaning are you ready to put in the work? If it is, your answers should motivate you to plan the changes you wish to make in your life.

Behavioral approaches are centered on the individual working to change their behaviors. Behavioral change techniques use reinforcement, punishment, shaping, modeling, and related techniques to alter behavior. These methods have the benefit of being highly focused, which means they can produce fast and effective results.

Leadership

Leadership Coaching

The definition of Leadership Coaching is a developmental process where a leader gets tailored help from a coach to help them achieve a goal and become a more effective leader.

Leadership coaching is "tailored to the individual," or rather, a bespoke development process for leaders that is achieved in partnership with a coach. The coach's role is that of ally who, from the outset, believes that the leader has unlimited potential to achieve the goal or outcome that they have set for themselves.

The coach's role is to help remove the obstacles that stand in the way of the leader attaining their goals. This is achieved through careful questioning and deep listening. The coach steps into the world of the coachee while maintaining a careful distance of objectivity, whereby they can gradually help the leader work through whatever is in the way of achieving the objective (either mental or emotional hurdles, such as beliefs, habits or fears). Through a process of inviting introspection and self-reflection, the coach helps the coachee clear a path for success.

5 Benefits of Leadership Coaching

Leadership coaching can have many benefits for individuals as well as the organizations they are a part of. Here are five of those benefits:

1. *Enhanced Performance*

   Leadership coaching can help leaders more accurately examine their weak points, gain better perspective about their abilities and how to better make use of them.

2. *Empowerment*

   Working with an executive coach can help those in leadership positions learn how to empower themselves and those on their teams. This has the added benefit of increasing team member's engagement in opportunities to collaborate.

3. *A fresh perspective*

We do not know what we cannot see. Having an outside perspective can be extremely powerful when looking to make meaningful and lasting changes.

4. *Confidence*

Having a coach's support while making meaningful changes, as well as celebrating their wins, can positively impact a leader's confidence levels.

5. *Job and life satisfaction*

By taking the time to step back and clearly assess their lives with the help of a coach, leaders can find more time for work/life balance. This tends to lead to better performance, retention, and increased satisfaction with their job.

What can you learn through leadership coaching?

The benefits mentioned above can be powerful and impactful, but it's also worth looking at how individuals can learn and grow from leadership development coaching.

1. *Self-awareness*

Self-awareness is one of the top growth areas of any type of coaching. We all have blind spots and while a leader may be satisfied with his own performance, others on the team may see it differently. The reverse can be true as well — the leader may be too self-critical or suffer imposter syndrome while others think she is doing fine.

Or perhaps the leader is mostly doing well, but there are specific behaviors or thoughts that are clouding their perspective or making them less effective than they might be. They might not recognize how a belief or mindset is affecting their approach or being felt by the team.

By developing awareness about automatic thoughts and myriad other behaviors, thoughts, and feelings, the leader can start to have a different engagement with themselves, their team, and others in their life.

2. Communication style

Building a higher degree of self-awareness around your communication skills, both verbal and nonverbal, can be a game-changer. It's easy for leaders to overlook communication as a skillset — at least, until the need becomes obvious. Perhaps it's a new situation (e.g., a company transformation) or an interpersonal challenge (e.g., a toxic team member). In either case, leaders may find that their usual communication style doesn't get the intended results.

Coaching a leader to communicate more effectively can include setting clear expectations, offering constructive feedback, or even shifting a leader's nonverbal communication. Additionally, leadership coaching can help leaders create a more inclusive and supportive environment for their teams by examining the language they use with others.

3. Listening skills

Are you listening well? (Hint: if you don't know, ask). Are you hearing what others are saying or merely waiting until the person across from you stops talking so that you can talk? Good leadership involves more listening than most would think.

By honing one's listening skills and being attuned to others, leaders can unlock a wide range of potential benefits for themselves and their teams. A coach can aid in developing communication and active listening skills that can be invaluable when leading teams.

4. Self-regulation

Leaders do not exist in a vacuum. Rather they are constantly interacting with others, and it has an impact. In fact, we know from our own data and others that these day-to-day interactions with one's manager have the greatest impact on direct reports' sense of belonging and inclusion, job satisfaction, and empowerment. So when a leader can't regulate their emotions, it can cloud their own judgment and negatively affect the environment and experience for everyone else.

Effective leadership coaching can help a leader to become better at regulating their own emotional responses.

By identifying ways to step back, they give themselves the opportunity to calm down and re-engage in a more productive conversation. Learning to self-regulate may include identifying patterns and potential triggers to decrease their impact on the leader and their team. Even naming the emotion that is present can go a long way towards helping one better manage their responses to various situations.

5. *Growth mindset*

Leadership coaching can help individuals unlock a growth mindset, as opposed to a fixed one. With this type of mindset, leaders can see obstacles as opportunities for growth, not something to be dreaded or feared. Being flexible, bouncing back from setbacks, and thinking creatively is a powerful skill to develop.

Some of the most effective leaders of the last several generations demonstrate an ability to think holistically and a commitment to growth. When challenges occurred, they didn't think of them as roadblocks. Instead, they looked for growth opportunities for their product, business, or team.

6. *Cultivate empathy*

Ever heard the saying, "No one cares what you know until they know how much you care?" This is essentially about empathy. Leaders who readily tap into empathy for others are generally more effective in their roles. When an employee is struggling, senior leaders can provide value just by seeing their pain and acknowledging it.

In turn, this allows employees to see leaders as a safe place to speak their truth when they are feeling particularly stuck or challenged. It is not necessarily for the leader to solve the issue, but rather to look for understanding and ways to better support their employees in trying times.

7. *Leverage strengths*

Leadership coaches are particularly adept at helping others to see the strengths they bring to the table. Not in the way that one might answer an interview question, but a real examination of what a coachee's strengths are and how to best leverage them. Strengths are often specific to the individual. With the help of a coach, a leader can put their particular strengths to use in unique and unexpected ways.

8. *Executive presence*

More than just a buzzword, executive presence is about how a leader communicates, shows up for others, and how they generally present themselves to the world. A leadership coach can help each individual leader gain insight into what their current personal brand is and how to work towards making both big and subtle changes to achieve the most effective executive presence possible.

Leadership coaching is a powerful management training tool to help business leaders at all levels leverage the leadership skills within themselves to maximize performance. It helps you increase awareness through practice and straightforward feedback. You'll sharpen your inherent leadership skills to better motivate teams and deliver specific personal, professional and organizational goals.

> **Leadership is not about titles, positions, or work hours.**
> **It's about relationships.**
>
> *–Jim Kouzes*

How to Develop Into a Leader

For the longest time, we have entertained the concept of some people being "born leaders," coming into this world gifted with the characteristics of one who is able to lead and motivate.

However, as time went by, we found out more about human behavior and the extent of man's capabilities. While some exceptional people may have been born with the knack for leadership, most leaders are actually made and not born.

Theories on Leadership

The idea that leaders are "born and not made" was presented in two theories. First is the Trait Theory of leadership, which states that people are born inherited leadership traits, and that if they have the right combination and the right amount of these traits, they are destined to become good, even great, leaders.

The Great Man Theory took the same stance, saying that being a leader is something that one is born with, and his greatness as a leader will come out when it is greatly needed. This theory even attached a degree of mysticism to the personality of a leader, who just "magically appears" when there is a need for him.

Of course, behavioral theorists eventually came out to refute this, taking the other side of the argument by saying that anyone can become a good leader if he undergoes a learning process. Leadership is not something that is inherited and embedded in the genes, because it can be acquired and learned through perception, teaching, training, practice and experience, over a long period of time.

As discussed by Brigette Hyacinth, author of *The Edge of Leadership: A Leader's Handbook for Success*, leadership is an ART, more than a SCIENCE. It is also a matter of timing, and there is a great degree of dependence on certain factors such as the environment, location, and other external forces. Most of the time, leadership is also a choice.

While she agrees that leadership is comprised of a set of traits and qualities that are innate in the individual, these traits and qualities are stimulated, refined and perfected through both formal and informal education, training, learning and experience. At the end of the day, the individual will decide whether to be a leader or not.

Most theorists reconciled the two sides of the leadership coin by saying that leaders are partly born and partly made. In any case, there is an unspoken acknowledgement that leadership – or at least parts or aspects of it – is learned. In structured environments, leadership programs are institutionalized. One of the initiatives included in such programs is leadership coaching, now seen as one of the most essential tools for personal and professional development.

How to Improve Leadership Skills

Empower and inspire others. Learn to follow. Be humble. Have a genuine concern for others. Celebrate accomplishments and learn from failure. Be a Peacekeeper and solve conflict. As you can see, if you want to develop your leadership skills, there is more than one way to go about it. Below you will find some of the best methods you should consider.

1. *Do something you are passionate about*

   One of the most crucial parts about being a leader is the ability to motivate others to want to succeed. Instilling that burning desire and drive in another worker can be a fulfilling experience, but it is by no means an easy feat.

   The truth is, people can tell when you are here for the pay and not because the project is something you truly care about. Only by working in afield you are passionate about will you become one of the best leaders around. Ultimately, you need to show your own burning passion for the job to make others also want to succeed.

2. Take management and leadership courses

Most leadership skills are a type of soft skill rather than hard skills. To understand the difference, the main way to determine if a skill is hard or soft is asking if it can be taught or dissected into different skill levels.

For example, a hard skill like coding can be taught and some coders have higher certification than others. Whereas a soft skill like problem solving is not often taught and there are no recognized levels of problem-solving skills.

However, research has found that this is not always the case. Some soft skills often associated with leadership can be taught through structured learning and short courses. These courses can increase the individual's awareness of their own behaviors and what is required, unlocking the potential to improve their leadership skills over time. Moreover, these courses can help us to understand the theory behind different leadership styles.

An example of these leadership development courses is the popular Management and Leadership Personal Development Course. However, many more courses are available on our dedicated management course page.

3. Consider every day as an opportunity

Because leadership skills are mostly based around soft skills, every single day you have an opportunity to develop many of the same skills that leaders need. From ordering a coffee at a local café to discussing a project in a team meeting, you can hone you listening, public speaking and many other skills associated with leadership.

Most of the time, we carry out these social interactions without even thinking and with minimal effort. By becoming more aware of them and seeing them as an opportunity to develop, we can be proactive in developing simple skills that go a long way for the best leaders.

4. *Brush up on your hard skills*

   We just discussed how most leadership skills are soft skills, so why would we tell you to brush up on your hard skills? The answer is quite simple.

   Members of a team will look to their leader when they get stuck on a task and don't know what to do next. These team members expect their leaders to be able to provide effective solutions based on their knowledge and expertise. If they cannot, or frequently fail to impress, the team can lose confidence in them as a leader.

   For that reason, a leader does need to have excellent hard skills and knowledge related to the overall project. Equipped with expert hard skills, their team's confidence in them as a leader will be maintained and they may even have more appreciation or admiration for them.

   The other benefit – not to be overlooked – is that specialist knowledge will increase the confidence of the leader to guide the team to success.

5. *Personal reflection*

   If you have committed to improving leadership skills and have taken on some of the methods listed above, it is paramount that you incorporate some personal reflection time into your weekly routine. Reflecting on specific situations and how you handled them will enable you to identify areas for improvement and what you could have done better.

   Only by reflecting on situations can you be prepared when a similar situation comes around again. The key takeaway is that there is no such thing as a perfect leader and everyone in a senior role should be reflecting on their work and targeting ways to improve how they lead a team.

6. *Find a mentor*

   If you have a leader in your life who you would like to learn from, you can ask them to mentor you. If they already do this well, it's likely they have put time and thought into leadership and reflected on what works well for them. This is a great way to both learn leadership skills and get feedback on your strengths and weaknesses from somebody who can help you work on them.

   The prospect of advancing to the top of one's field is what makes it possible for many people to keep plugging away at their jobs, honing their skills, and taking on new projects. But after a certain point, career development depends on more than technical skills and a willingness to work hard. You also need soft skills, not the least of which is the ability to take on a leadership role.

   Some people are natural leaders, but anyone can develop the skill set needed with some practice. Lastly, a major characteristic of being a leader is having confidence, not only in others, but in your own skills and capabilities to lead other people and lead them well.

Becoming a Leadership and Life Coach

Becoming a great Life and Leadership Coach require a number of personal qualities and extensive training, supervision, and experience.

Appropriate qualities include openness, approachability, curiosity, and empathy. The quality and price of training differ as much as those of operating coaches.

> **"Any time you sincerely want to make a change,**
> **the first thing you must do is to raise your standards."**
>
> *–Anthony Robbins,*
> *Awaken the Giant Within*

Life coaching sessions are usually based on a coaching model, such as the GROW model, and have a firm structure. They begin with a brief description of the problem, determine the desired session outcome, and then work through the individual steps of the chosen model.

And life coaching clients can be of (nearly) all ages and walks of life. They may approach a coach when seeking guidance to work through a complex problem or looking for clarity about important life decisions and direction.

Relevant life areas can span across all domains including relationships, career, health, finance, personal development, and leisure.

Coaching in a business environment is a training method in which a more experienced or skilled individual provides an employee with advice and guidance intended to help develop the individual's skills, performance, and career.

Coaching is a highly individualized process that depends on both the nature of the client and the coach's knowledge, skills and abilities. However, coaches have several recognized techniques and tools to draw on in almost any coaching situation.

As organizations have come to recognize the many purposes and benefits of coaching, the field has grown dramatically, and some organizations actively work to create a culture of coaching. A coaching culture within an organization includes more than formal coaching; it is a culture in which coaching behaviors are used as a means of communicating, managing and influencing others. It is also an environment that values learning and the development of employees.

Coaching should be approached like any other strategic goal. Successful execution requires commitment from the organization and the person being coached, a plan to obtain results, qualified coaches, and a follow-up evaluation. Today, it is possible to obtain training and certification in the coaching field. As a career path, coaching usually involves independent consulting, although some large organizations employ coaches on their regular staff.

Techniques and Tools

At its best, coaching is about partnering rather than about one person being "the expert" and lecturing the other. The client is the expert in the organization; the coach helps the client develop a higher level of expertise. The coach can use a variety of methods to facilitate the coaching process:

- Using data from anonymous 360-degree surveys or climate analysis surveys to identify objective behaviors that can be linked with business outcomes. CEOs are very often shocked at the disparity in their rating and their subordinates' ratings of them. This might be the first awareness that they are out of touch.

- Using personality and behavioral assessments to diagnose which traits and behaviors are dominant or lacking, and which might be easy or difficult to change.

- Listening actively; the coach does not solve the client's problems—the client solves his or her own problems.

- Helping clients distinguish what is important from what is not.

- Leading clients outside of their comfort zone.

- Acknowledging the client's accomplishments and empathizing (not sympathizing) when the client is down.

- Providing perspective based on the coach's own experiences.

- Helping the client set goals, develop an action plan for moving ahead, and anticipate and overcome potential obstacles.

- Recommending specific books or other sources of learning.

- Encouraging journaling to gain awareness of emotions and behaviors and to track progress toward goals.

- Participating in role-playing and simulations to promote skill practice.

- Meeting on a regular basis, with on-the-job "homework" assignments between meetings.

- Managing the confidentiality of the coaching partnership. In most cases, the official client is the organization paying the coaching invoice, yet the true client is the individual being coached.

- Designing systems to track the return on investment of coaching.

The GROW model was popularized in the coaching industry by Sir John Whitmore in his 1992 book *Coaching for Performance: GROWing Human Potential and Purpose.*

Whitmore's acronym stands for:

Goals.

Reality, or current reality.

Options.

Way forward, or what you will do.

Coaching Applications

The growth of the corporate coaching industry has been rapid. Similar to personal training in the private realm, coaching in the business environment is quickly becoming mainstream and branching out to all areas of organizational management. Coaching can be an effective tool in meeting numerous organizational needs.

Training and Certification

A successful coaching career requires a combination of skills, credentials, experience and business acumen. To qualify for a regular position as an executive coach, a person might well need to have a graduate degree in organizational development or leadership development.

Numerous organizations provide certification in the coaching competency, including:

- *International Coach Federation.* Based in Lexington, Kentucky, this nonprofit federation is described as the largest worldwide resource for business and personal coaches and as a source for those who are seeking a coach. It offers a Master Certified Coach credential.

- *Worldwide Association of Business Coaches.* This Canada-based organization for the business coaching industry serves and develops the U.S., Canadian and overseas business coaching markets.

- *College of Executive Coaching.* This California-based institution provides personal and executive coach training, coaching services, and leadership development programs to professionals.

- *National Career Development Association (NCDA).* A division of the American Counseling Association, the NCDA, based in Broken Arrow, Okla., provides services to the public and to professionals involved with or interested in career development, including professional development activities, publications, research, public information, professional standards, advocacy and recognition for achievement and service.

- *Center for Creative Leadership.* This nonprofit institution, with offices in San Diego, Calif., Colorado Springs, Colo., and Greensboro, NC, focuses exclusively on leadership. It integrates research with training, coaching, assessment and publishing for leaders and organizations.

- *Center for Coaching Certification.* This Florida-based organization offers business, career, executive, life and wellness coach training and coaching certification opportunities.

- *Masterpiece Coaching Institute.* This Virginia-based organization founded by this Author offers life and leadership coach training and coaching certification opportunities with a focus on values, cultural competence, evidenced based theories, skills, and transformational leadership.

Conclusion

Conclusion

Corporate leadership development and training is critical to any organization that wants to dominate its industry. With the rapid pace of change in the business landscape, companies need to find a sustainable strategy to continuously develop new leaders and enhance the skills of the current ones.

As you can see, there are many options to get training in life and leadership coaching. Whether you are ready to practice as a life coach is up to your own judgment, standards, and expectations. While cheaper and quicker training routes may be tempting, remember the profession comes with responsibilities and implications for your clients.

When done right, life coaching can be an incredibly rewarding career that can provide life-changing insights for clients.

Once you are skilled enough to guide your clients through mental roadblocks and get to witness a genuine 'a-ha moment,' you will appreciate your financial and time investment in good-quality training.

A successful life and leadership training program is rooted in a strong culture of learning and sharing knowledge. The rest is getting clear on who you are, who you want to be, and the difference you want to make on the world

"Great leaders don't set out to be a leader.
They set out to make a difference.
It's never about the role-always about the goal."

—Lisa Haisha

References

Chapter 3

Ford, B. Q., Shallcross, A. J., Mauss, I. B., Floerke, V. A., & Gruber, J. (2014). Desperately seeking happiness: Valuing happiness is associated with symptoms and diagnosis of depression. *Journal of social and clinical psychology*, *33*(10), 890-905.

Hill, P. L., Burrow, A. L., Brandenberger, J. W., Lapsley, D. K., & Quaranto, J. C. (2010). Collegiate purpose orientations and well-being in early and middle adulthood. *Journal of Applied Developmental Psychology*, *31*(2), 173-179.

Mike Ward (M.Div.). What Is God's Purpose For Your Life (And How To Find It). (2017, January 17). https://www.cornerstone.edu/blog-post/what-is-gods-purpose-for-your-life-and-how-to-find-it/

Chapter 4

Hofstede, G. J., Pedersen, P. B., & Hofstede, G. (2002). *Exploring culture: Exercises, stories, and synthetic cultures*. Nicholas Brealey.

Schein, E. H. (2010). *Organizational culture and leadership* (Vol. 2). John Wiley & Sons.

Williams, B. (2001). Accomplishing cross cultural competence in youth development programs. *Journal of Extension*, *39*(6), 1-6.

Wilson, J., Ward, C., & Fischer, R. (2013). Beyond culture learning theory: What can personality tell us about cultural competence? *Journal of cross-cultural psychology*, *44*(6), 900-927.

Chapter 6

Weigl, R.C. (2009). *International Journal of Intercultural Relations*, 33: 4.

Hays, P.A. (2008). Addressing Cultural Complexities in Practice: Assessment, Diagnosis, and Therapy. American Psychological Association.

Chapter 7

Park, N., Peterson, C. Szvarca, D. Vander Molen, R.J., Kim, E.S., & Collon, K. (2014). Positive Psychology and Physical Health. https://www.ncbi.nlm.nih.gov/pmc/articles/PMC6124958/#:~:text=Researchers%20have%20shown%20that%20positive,meditation%20can%20boost%20immune%20function.

Chapter 8

Early, G. Embracing the contribution of both behavioral and cognitive theories to cognitive behavioral therapy: Maximizing the richness. *Clinical Social Work Journal.* 2016;45(1):39-48. doi:10.1007/s10615-016-0590-5

Lungu, A., Boone, M.S., Chen, S.Y., Chen, C.E., & Walser, R.D. (2021, January 8). Effectiveness of a Cognitive Behavioral Coaching Program Delivered via Video in Real World Settings. https://www.ncbi.nlm.nih.gov/pmc/articles/PMC7815061/

Chapter 11

Asnaani, H, Vonk J.J., Sawyer, A.T., Fang, A. The efficacy of cognitive behavioral therapy: a review of meta-analyses. (2012). *Cognitive Therapy and Research,* 36(5), 427-440. doi:10.1007/s10608-012-9476-1

Chapter 12

Clear, J. (2018). Atomic Habits. SI: Random House.

Early, G. Embracing the contribution of both behavioral and cognitive theories to cognitive behavioral therapy: Maximizing the richness. *Clinical Social Work Journal.* 2016;45(1):39-48. doi:10.1007/s10615-016-0590-5

Knell, S.M. & Dasari, M. Cognitive-behavioral play therapy for anxiety and depression. (2016). *Empirically based play interventions for children (2nd ed)*. Published online, pp. 77-94. doi:10.1037/14730-005

Lungu, A., Boone, M.S., Chen, S.Y., Chen, C.E., & Walser, R.D. (2021, January 8). Effectiveness of a Cognitive Behavioral Coaching Program Delivered via Video in Real World Settings. https://www.ncbi.nlm.nih.gov/pmc/articles/PMC7815061/

Tolin D.F. (2016). *Doing CBT : A Comprehensive Guide to Working with Behaviors, Thoughts, and Emotions*. The Guilford Press.